A Career in Coding

Careers in Computers

I0812963

Rory McCallum

COMPUTER SCIENCE For the REAL World™

Rosen Classroom™

Published in 2018 by The Rosen Publishing Group, Inc.
29 East 21st Street, New York, NY 10010

Book Design: Jennifer Ryder-Talbot
Editor: Caitie McAneney

Photo Credits: Cover, 8 sabrisy/Shutterstock.com; p. 4 ronstik/Shutterstock.com; p. 6 dotshock/Shutterstock.com; p. 10 Rawpixel.com/Shutterstock.com; p. 12 ESB Professional/Shutterstock.com; p. 14 GaudiLab/Shutterstock.com.

ISBN: 9781538352519
6-pack ISBN: 9781508136958

Manufactured in the United States of America

CPSIA Compliance Information: Batch #WS18RC: For Further Information contact Rosen Publishing, New York, New York at 1-800-237-9932

Table of Contents

What Do Programmers Do?

Do you want a **career** in coding? Computer programmers work with code as part of their job. They create programs that make a computer do certain tasks. They also fix code that has problems in it.

Programmers work for many different kinds of companies. Some work for companies that create software, or computer programs, for many different **industries**. Every industry, from education to medicine, needs software.

Problem-Solving Masters

Do you like to solve problems? We solve problems in our lives every day. Some problems are so small that we don't even realize we're solving them.

Programmers are masters of solving problems. First, programmers must figure out what the problem or **challenge** is. Then, they try to fix it one step at a time. Breaking down a problem makes it easier to solve.

gridHeights()
$(window).resize(
gridHeights()
})
$('.close-
$(this).closest(
return
})
$('#contact-form').
success: function
alert(data.message)
console.log(form)
if (data.status ==
$(form).resetForm()
}
}
})
').isotope({
// options
itemSelector: 'li',
layoutMode: 'fitRows'
})
').imagesLoc
').isot

Code Creators

Sometimes programmers have to create new code. They need to know the right computer language for the job. Computer languages make it possible to tell a computer what to do. There are many different computer languages.

Programmers who create code have to first look at their **project** as a whole. Then, they have to break it down into smaller steps. They think about different questions. What does this program have to do? What will the different parts of the program be?

Teamwork

Programmers sometimes work alone. Some work from home. However, programmers often work together as a team. They share ideas and parts of code to help each other solve problems. They may **brainstorm** different ways to approach building a computer program.

When a team works together, members can finish a project much faster than if they worked alone. They can help each other find bugs, or mistakes, in a program.

Debugging

Computer code can be made up of long strings of letters and numbers. There are many ways code can have bugs in it.

Programmers often have to go back into a program and find the bugs. These bugs may mean the computer program doesn't work the way it's supposed to. This process is called debugging. Once programmers figure out where a bug is, they can fix the problem. Then the computer program will be up and running!

Does It Work?

What happens after a programmer creates or fixes a program? It's time to test the new code. The programmer will run the program to make sure it works correctly. Sometimes it doesn't work on the first try. Then, the programmer will fix the problem and try again.

A career in coding is great for someone who loves to solve problems and puzzles. Each day has a new challenge!

Glossary

brainstorm: To think of ideas or ways to solve a problem in a group.

career: A job someone does for a long time.

challenge: A test of abilities.

industry: A group of related businesses.

project: A task.

Index